VOLUME I

IN OUR HEARTS
FROM THE
START

DANETTA E. MCDAVID

~ 1 ~

IN OUR HEARTS FROM THE START

by Danetta McDavid

DEDICATION

***To my Lord and Savior, Jesus Christ*—** This book is my "yes" to You.

Thank You for calling me to this
journey, for guiding me every step, and for showing me that obedience
is not always easy, but always worth it. Every page is a reflection of
Your faithfulness, and it is my prayer that all glory returns to You.

***To the biological mother of our twins*—**

Your courage and obedience in entrusting us with two of your most
precious treasures changed all of our lives. Through your selfless "yes,"
God answered the prayer of a child in the most unique and miraculous
way. Your love and trust will forever be remembered.

***To my husband and our twins*—**

You have walked this journey beside me, sharing in the joys,
challenges, and miracles. To my husband, your love, patience, and
willingness to follow God's leading with me has been a gift I will never
take for granted. And to our precious twins, the joy, wonder, and love
you bring into our lives is beyond words. Always remember: you are
loved, you are more special than you know and most importantly you
were chosen.

***To our beautiful and loving family friend*—**

Thank you for being obedient to God when He spoke through you,
saying, "Those are your twins." That moment sent a shock wave
through my mind and forever changed the course of our lives. Your
faithfulness and courage were the spark that began this miraculous
journey.

This book is for all of you: a love letter to my family, a tribute to those
who obeyed God's call, and most importantly a testimony to His
perfect plan.

Table of Contents

Chapter 1: The Call that Changed Everything

W excited. Later, she called again, her tone carrying a hint hen she first called to tell me she was pregnant, I was

of arrogance.

"You always wanted twins, didn't you?" She asked

"Yes Ma'am." I replied, reluctantly.

"Well, I'm pregnant with twins. Can you believe it?"

I smiled and said, "That's awesome."

I was happy for her, yet there was a strange feeling I couldn't quite name. It wasn't sadness or anger—just something I couldn't explain.

After hanging up, I called a close family friend, who is a therapist and told her I needed to talk.

I started the conversation out with a strong "Oh My Goodness! God got jokes!"

In my mind I thought, *I've prayed for twins since I was in third grade, at the private school my mother chose for me.* But what I said was, "Guess who called me today? She called to tell me she was pregnant with twins, God really does have jokes" I said, "and here He is blessing yet another person I know with twins."

"Calm down," she said. "Those are your twins".

I shockingly replied "What? No way. That family would never allow it".

"Calm down," she repeated. "Just watch God work. He can bless you however He chooses. And yes, God is the best joke-teller."

I sighed. "Okay. I'll just trust the process."

When I told my husband about my conversation with the biological mom, he simply said "Just tell her congratulations," as if it wasn't a big deal. When I mentioned what my friend had said, his response was a brief, "Yeah okay". Not sure if he believed it.

Actually it's not okay, I'm in my emotions right now. I don't know how I'm feeling, I'm not mad, I'm not sad, I'm not irritated. Actually I just feel an extremely strange emotion.

****

Months later we were at work when the phone rang. My husband answered, his eyes going wide as he looked at me.

"She had the babies," he whispered.

I stared back, confused. "Who are we talking about?"

He told me and I froze mid-conversation with a client. "What's going on?" I asked.

He said she was upset and wanted me to take the call.

On the other line was a frantic crying young lady, "Could y'all please take the twins? They're not letting us take them home," she said.

My husband and I locked eyes, I told her to speak with their caseworker and have them call us. She insisted, "I don't want them with anyone else, I want them with you."

Another long stare passed between us until the call ended.

Chapter 2: The Meeting of Our Hearts

M appearances, conflicting stories from case workers, and onths passed, filled with conversations, court home inspections. All in preparation for the babies we hoped would complete our family. Or so we thought.

The day had finally come to meet the girls face-to-face after only seeing their pictures. We were all extremely excited.

Looking back on this time, since I was the one taking pictures and making sure everyone was comfortable and safe, this day will be a journey through my focused lens.

As we prepared to leave our home, our oldest son and daughter, my husband and myself quietly anticipating, the first gaze into these beautiful little faces.

We had to meet at a government location, which was fine. When we arrived we were instructed to have a seat in the waiting area. They finally called our name and the four of us were escorted into a room. I would consider the room extremely small, there were no pictures on the walls, the walls were a yellowish green in color and it felt emotionally cold.

The room held a desk and 3 chairs, the girls sat in their car seats on top of the desk while the case worker watched our son and daughter lift the seats to the floor in front of the chairs they'd chosen. The room was not large enough for all of us to comfortable fit.

After the case worker left, I stood in the doorway to get the best pictures. My husband pulled the last chair from behind the desk and sat. At one point my son offered me his seat so I could hold the babies, but I declined. Though, later I did get to hold and love on them before our visit ended.

I can't even put into words how we felt when we saw them. The look on my son's, daughter's, and my husband's faces was deeply emotional. My daughter immediately lifted Twin A from her car seat, which made me smile even more, especially since Twin A favored her a bit. My son picked up Twin B with the biggest grin I'd ever seen.

After helping them get settled, I took pictures of the four of them so we'd always remember the day we met.

Even now, over 12 years later, I still revisit those photos and the excitement they captured.

Oh, how precious they were. Just looking into their beautiful little faces melted our hearts.

Words cannot express how my husband and I felt watching our oldest two looking into the eyes of the little ones who could become our youngest. After a while my husband was given twin B and my daughter was still lovingly holding twin A. I must say, that was an amazingly awesome moment in time for us.

Although it was now time to say goodbye to the babies and head back home, we were hopeful we'd see them again. My husband and son carried the girls to their foster parent's vehicle while my daughter and I walked alongside, just so we could get a little more time.

A day or so later, we were a little sad, but still excited to have spent time with the babies. Shortly after that initial visit we were offered visitation with the girls, Sundays only.

Although we enjoyed our Sundays with the girls, which consisted of picking the girls up at the designated spot, going straight to church, after church most Sundays we'd go visit Momma, every once in a while we'd go out to dinner. We desired more time and more days with the girls.

The biological mom had also requested that they be placed with us, but for some reasons never explained, the caseworker refused.

After months of going to court, hours of updating our foster parenting classes, investigations, and coming in to inspect our home for Sunday visits, a different caseworker told us that the judge had already approved overnight visits from the very beginning. We were shocked.

With that knowledge I reached out to the foster parent informing her what we were told about the girls being allowed overnight visits, she admitted that she had known all along but "didn't think it would be best for them".

Shortly after this conversation during one of our drop offs, the foster parent told me her mom had come to live with them and had been diagnosed with dementia. I asked her wasn't that going to be a lot to handle with twin babies? I was stunned when she informed me, she was thinking about separating the girls.

I asked, "Why would you do that?"

She explained how she would keep the calm twin and get rid of the twin that was demanding and cried the loudest.

I was furious. I immediately called both caseworkers and a supervisor, leaving multiple messages. I told them there was no reason the girls should be separated. I must have called a dozen times before anyone responded.

Though it was disappointing, I believed God was at work throughout this whole situation, just as our family friend had said. We were unexpectedly happy when the weekly visits ended, though we were never told why. I've always had my thoughts. Some might wonder why we would be happy our only time with the girls came to an end when that's all we had with them?

Well on December 21, 2012, the babies came to live with us full-time. Although we were informed the girls would be going home with their biological parents once they complied with the recommendations of the state we were glad to help and more than happy to love on these innocent babies for the time being.

Chapter 3: From Panic to Peace

Fextremely trying time.

     riday, December 21, 2012 filled with excitement yet an

The day the babies were brought to our home was one of the most exciting yet trying days. I don't want to say of our lives, but I will say, it was extremely upsetting yet happy.

Not only were we notified two hours prior to their arrival and at the same time they were to arrive, my first client of the day was scheduled. She (the caseworker) dropped them off in their car seats with a plastic bag and a backpack. The girls were filthy, and in the plastic bag there were three cans of Similac, and in the backpack appeared to be dirty clothes that were way too small during my initial inspection.

She (the caseworker) might have stayed approximately 10 minutes or so with much attitude, before rushing off. In the midst of all of this my husband, and I were amazed to look upon these two precious faces of the most beautiful little angels my God could have created. They were wide awake. Looking at us as if to say, ***now what***?

I began looking through the bag, shocked to find a few pair of socks, four sleepers that actually were way too small for either of the girls, pacifiers and a couple of dirty T-shirts. What was not in either bag were Pampers or wipes.

I immediately called the caseworker to ask her had she forgotten the rest of their belongings.

She said "No I didn't, I picked them up from daycare and brought them straight to you," with a voice that was less than kind.

I began to let her know that they had no Pampers or wipes and only one bottle a piece. I also informed her, they had no clothes, and the sleepers that were in the bag looked to be way too small.

"What am I supposed to do about this, I have to go to work in less than an hour," I said.

"I brought what I was given. "They are your responsibility now," she exclaimed and hung up.

I go back into the family room to let my husband know how the conversation went. He became extremely nervous, anxious and somewhat overwhelmed at this point. As soon as my husband began to display those emotions, the girls began whining a bit.

We picked them up out of the car seats to cuddle them, and hopefully calm them down. Next thing you know little whining, turned into all-out crying. I checked them and yes, they were soaking wet. My husband began panicking at this point even more.

While I'm trying to calm him and the girls down I let him know, I had to go to the store real quick for Pampers and wipes.

He said, "We can't do this, our life is not conducive to babies. We work too much, we're never home, and we don't eat right." In his panic he found every excuse he could.

The fear on his face shocked me. We had cared for many godchildren before, so to me this was nothing new. I knew that if we stayed calm, the babies would stay calm. But if we panicked, they would too.

I sat beside him. "It's going to be all right. You can do this. We can do this." I said.

During this time the girls became extremely agitated. I said "OK Babe I need you to calm down. I need you to breathe."

"We can't do this. We can't take care of two babies at once. What are we going to do?" He said.

"Calm down, babe," I repeated. "Right now they are feeding off your nervous anxiety and anxious emotions. God would not choose this for us if we could not handle it."

Once he calmed down, the girls did too. He hugged and kissed them. "We're good. It's going to be all right."

They looked up at him and calmed right down, gave a big smile and I was off to the store.

I hurriedly went to Family Dollar for the necessities needed since that's the closest store to us to get us through until we can make a real run to the store.

When I got back home, I bathed the girls and got them all cleaned up. Thank God this was my last day at work until after the New Year. After they had fallen asleep, my husband and I prayed and then I was off to work. My clients are the best; they understood everything going on and were willing to let me push appointments back so I could come in later.

While at work, I couldn't wait to get back home to my babies. Yes, I said my babies, I just can't explain the bond and love that God had already placed in my heart for them.

While at work, I wrote our first baby list of all the necessary items they needed. And since Christmas and our anniversary were days away, what an awesome gift God had blessed us with, I couldn't wait to go shopping for them. I couldn't wait to shower these two beautiful angels with the love I know that only God could have given us to extend to them.

Chapter 4: Looking Like Daddy

Ffor the babies, God's plan was already in motion; even among rom the moment we received the call asking if we could care

our staff and clients. The excitement and support were overwhelming.

Our first baby shower was held in the salon. The girls moved from one set of loving arms to another, and I don't recall either of them crying. They seemed as overjoyed as we were. It was amazing to be surrounded by so much love and so many people eager to welcome these two beautiful babies into our lives and home.

In the midst of the joy and happiness, I began to think of my third grade prayer request. My mom had taken me out of public school and transferred me to a private school and there you pray every day so in third grade, my first year there in Bible class they asked the question. ***Does anyone have a prayer request?***

My prayer request way back then was not only to get married before Jesus returned. I also asked God for twins.

Funny thing is I really wanted twins. However, I knew in the scheme of things I had to ask for a husband first since I was always taught that was the order of things and here we are celebrating what has come to be known as OUR twins.

Although some might say, "That's not what you meant back then."

I've learned, when you pray for something and you have faith to receive it, God is the only one who knows how to best bring that prayer to reality. There's not a day that goes by that we don't thank Him for this awesome blessing and unique opportunity.

As that baby shower ended, another one appeared on the horizon, bringing family from church and beyond together to love on the girls.

At this second shower, someone said for the first time that Baby B looked like my husband. After the initial surprise, I explained they were both just a little full in the face. But as time went on, we heard it more and more: "She looks like your husband."

I believe baby A and B were now accustomed to extra love and extra attention. They smiled and laughed themselves right to sleep at this shower.

I thank God for doing all things well. Only God can cause baby girls to look like their dad to be in such a short time.

Chapter 5: We Chose You

A needed for day-to-day with six month old babies, it's time to fter getting ourselves together and picking up the necessities

go Christmas shopping.

What do you get for these beautiful blessings who have unknowingly given me everything I could ask for, as we celebrate 12 years anniversary together and our 2012 Christmas?

In addition to educational toys, our gift to them was holding them and loving on them for the entire holiday weekend. It actually never ends. Although at this point in time, we understand the mission is to bring reunification to the biological parents and the girls while caring for them. Every minute that passes forms a loving bond that will never be broken between us and the girls.

Every now and again my husband would say "We can't do this, or our life isn't conducive to twin babies. We work too much, we don't eat right, we're always gone or going somewhere."I listened to him, but in my heart, I always heard God say, *I have chosen you*.

And in God choosing us, we are more than able to do what needs to be done for our older son & daughter as well as these beautiful babies.

I had a client who has twins, a son and a daughter. She told me that I was special and I was blessed. She always told me that my four should always know how blessed they are. She would often tell me that and I just smiled and always said thank you.

Finally, one day I asked "Why, why do you say that so often?"

She begins to explain to me how she was pregnant twice, she has an older son in addition to her twins, and she gave birth to them. She loves them dearly and wouldn't exchange them for anything.

But, she said, God had chosen them for her. She hadn't chosen to be their parent; she simply became one.

"But you chose them," she told me. "One by one. When they were brought to you, you could have said no; that you and your husband were enjoying life without more responsibilities. But you said yes.

"And if you didn't tell anyone they weren't your biological children, no one would know. They even favor you and your husband; in looks, in attitudes, and in actions."

"I watch how you interact with them," she continued. "You and your husband love them with every fiber of your being. Not that parents don't love that way, but it's different; and it's a blessing to see someone love like that after choosing to love. If that makes sense."

"It does," I told her. "I completely understand."

After she told me that I had so much to think about because I never thought about it like that. We have always loved in spite of. And children did not ask to be here so why not love them and show them you care, and do your best by them.

When we spoke again she added "The attention you give them is beautiful. There are parents who have biological children that don't give the love and dedication you give these four children you chose."

I was so touched by all that she said. I thanked her from the bottom of my heart and asked God to help us to never give less than our best.

After letting my husband know our conversation, he began to nod his head and said he was glad I sincerely thanked her.

As time went on, and we became more and more comfortable in the role of parents of infants, we began paying attention to other parents, whether in the mall, in the salon, at the family functions or even at the day care we chose to allow our babies to attend.

And the observation my husband came up with was after numerous compliments on how blessed the children in our care are and how much love is seen in our dealings with them. He began to notice the difference in how we cherish these children, being individuals that for whatever reason have never birthed a child, and the way those who have birthed children are.

He said (biological) parents, at least some of the parents he's observed who have birth children, saw it as being able to birth a child was easy, somewhat nothing major, and they could just go have another one if they want to. They don't cherish and or appreciate their child/children as the blessing that they truly are.

And couples like us cherish and appreciate our gifts from heaven on a daily basis. We will pass up events with no worries to stay home with our gifts. We love spending time with our children, regularly sitting around talking, listening and or watching TV together.

There's been times we couldn't locate a sitter because we're not just going to let anyone watch over our children for an outing, and instead of continuing the search or allowing our blessings to be watched by a random person, we stay home and have an awesome evening with our children. I feel like we hold ourselves to a higher standard of accountability than some who actually gave birth. For us accountability, at its core, means striving to make not only the biological parents proud, but, more importantly, to honor God by lovingly nurturing the blessings He's given us.

Chapter 6: Loving Her for Letting Go

O most times she'd ask how the twins are. She would ask if n occasions the biological mom would call me. Although

she could come to my business to have her hair done. She is now an adult with children of her own, even though years ago she was also one of my babies.

I would always do my best to speak life into her as well as let her know I loved her. She would always end our call and or time together by thanking me for treating her like a real person.

My response was always the same. "You are a real person, remember I know you. You will always be my baby."

At the end of the day, I have always and will always love the biological mom. How can you not love someone who loves their children so much, that instead of taking them down the rocky road she may have to travel, she makes the decision to call someone she not only trusts but she loves to care for her most prized possessions. I believe with all my heart that God placed us on her heart in her time of despair for His reason and His purpose. The reason and purpose only God knows. I daily pray for her and thank God for her obedience in making that call which we are forever grateful.

In order to continue working in our business, we were in search of a daycare that the both of us trusted and saw fit for the girls to attend and continue to learn and grow.

While we were taking on a roller coaster ride by DSS, when trying to get financial assistance for daycare, my husband decided to stay home with the girls while I went to work.

Although I totally understood when I returned home from work, the girls no longer paid me much attention anymore. It was all about my husband. And oh how I loved that. I loved watching my husband's bond with the girls. I loved watching how much the girls were falling in love with my husband and watching him care for them on a daily basis. It was amazing.

We finally found the daycare where our little ones would be cared for. I had taken the tour of the facility, spoken to multiple employees, as well as parents who were dropping off and or picking up their children. It was settled. We were in love with the daycare we had found, and the level of care they would be giving to the girls.

Now comes one of the roller coaster rides I mentioned earlier. After a couple of weeks or so we decided to create a space in our business for the girls. After all, I was missing out on so much. And I missed them. I had always envisioned being able to stay home with our children for a couple years or even creating a place in my business for them. And here's the opportunity to do just that. In the center of the business we built a gated community with padded flooring for the girls.

We had to do what we had to do, since it seemed like we may not be given daycare vouchers. However, lo and behold, five months later vouchers were approved.

We were given a portion of the amount charged at the daycare. We would be responsible for the remaining balance of a little over $400 a week. We continued to see God's hand in every step of the plans carried out for the girls. This daycare was amazing. Their teachers were so impressed with the girls.

When we picked them up, they would thank us for having the sweetest babies ever, they'd say. We'd always smile and thank them. Once we got to know the teachers and saw that the girls seemed to be treated a little differently than the other children, I began asking questions.

They replied, "Your babies don't act anything like the other little ones we care for."

"Your girls listen, they can count, they know their colors, as well as say thank you and please. When they are told not to do something, they don't cry and fall out."

"We love them."

In my mind I'm thinking that's normal. All little kids, whose parents work with them know colors, know their numbers, they're polite. I'm thinking that's normal. They quickly let me know. It was not normal and they thought it was great which in a sense, showered our babies with favor (the favor of God).

We were told at nap time Baby A would lay right down and go to sleep no fuss no muss she was out every time shortly after her head hit the mat. This is exactly how she is at home. She was my busybody baby. Into everything, which made her tired I suppose.

On the other hand when her sister was put down for a nap, she lay down, but she was not going to sleep. She'd watch what was going on around her, she'd play little games with her fingers, but taking a nap during nap time was not happening. Their teachers were so impressed. They said every other child if they weren't falling asleep, they were causing problems. They would get up and leave the mat, disturb other children, cry, scream, and holler, but never quietly lay there like Twin B.

At every turn we saw God's hands on them. Although I believe when our family friend had told me over a year ago, and I was trusting God to do what only he could do. At this point, I was wondering God is this really how this is going to be an answered prayer of a third grader? After all, my husband and I were asked to care for these children until their biological parents complied with the cleanup orders from DSS so they could be taken home. Although the girls were thriving here with us and in daycare, there was an ugly weekly storm brewing in their little lives.

Chapter 7: The Painful Visits

A the biological parents were given the permission to visit. pproximately three months after being placed in our home,

They set them up for Saturdays, they were scheduled to pick the girls up and take them for the day and bring them back, at least that was the court order.

However, I will never forget the very first visit, which had me upset with the negative comments that were used to describe the girls. They never came at the time agreed to. Now and again I remind myself we are here to help facilitate reunification at this point.

They walked into our business, the three beautiful siblings and the biological parents. We had their car seats ready, and their bag packed with everything needed for hours of quality time. The siblings would always call them by name and the biological mother would call them twins. The first acknowledgment I heard from the biological father's mouth was extremely harsh. Describing how they looked. Their complexion, and then goes and sit down in the waiting area. Although the biological mother sat down in the same chairs, she told the girls she loved them while looking so detached. After she greeted them and sat down she looked as though she was done. The siblings were extremely excited about seeing the girls.

They sat there for approximately 10 minutes. I went over and asked if they were taking them to spend time with them?

They hesitantly replied, "ohyeah."

He walked outside, the siblings carried the bag and some toys, while my husband carried the girls to the vehicle and secured them in. Again, in my heart and my mind I keep telling myself we are keeping the girls safe until they are reunited with the biological parents.

My husband was quite disappointed when he came back in. We had to pray for the girls safety and protection again. My clients were dumbfounded after watching what had transpired during the pickup.

When they brought the girls back they smelled horrible. You would have thought the girls smoked. Their noses were running, they were congested. I was so sad for them.

A couple of days later, I took the girls to see their pediatrician and it was documented they were having an allergic reaction to cigarette smoke. I emailed the paperwork to the case worker as well as called to let her know.

She spoke to me as if there was nothing she could do. I asked her to please ask them not to smoke around the girls during their visits.

As time went on the visits got shorter. I remember them bringing the girls back looking as though they've been rolling in dirt, their Pampers seemed like they had not been changed in hours. Instead of milk in their bottles, they came back with lemonade in their bottles. We were in shock. The older the girls got the less they wanted to go with them. Next thing I know Saturday visits were over.

We were relieved. Until we got a call from the caseworker that there would be a transporter who would pick the girls up from daycare and take them for a 2 hour visit with the biological parents.

I was led to believe it was at their home. For the life of me, I could not understand why DSS would force parents who have shown no interest in their children to frequently visit them. However, they made the girls go.

After the first visit, my husband and I were called to the daycare when the girls got back from their visits. The girls would be so upset, crying so hard in the beginning it was from the time the transporter took them to the biological parents until they were brought back to the daycare. The girls would be so upset, crying uncontrollably. Their little faces were swollen, voices raspy and hoarse, all from being upset and purposefully, made to visit strangers. (In their little eyes)

After a few visits the girls would cry as soon as they saw the transporter as they would leave the daycare with someone other than us. Due to the girls being so upset, we decided to rearrange our schedules so we'd arrive to the daycare before the girls were picked up.

The transporter actually took my number to call so we could be at the daycare as soon as they arrived. It was so bad. The transporter told the caseworker it was torture for these babies.

"Why didn't you just not take them" I asked the transporter.

"I would lose my job." They responded.

This went on for weeks. We felt helpless. All we could do is continue to pray. Even in the bad times God has a plan. These innocent babies, who did not ask to be here, are being put through this torture. Although we made numerous complaints, they were ignored. And next thing we know these visits ended. Just like that. Neither Daycare nor we were ever told why. But God!

The girls were approximately 11 months when we picked them up from daycare one evening, and as we're putting on their coats Twin A said "Thank you Daddy" and Twin B said "Thank you Mommy" after we zipped them up and said "Okay let's go."

We looked at each other and said "What did you say?"

They repeated it as if it were nothing. I quickly called the teacher over to us and before we could get it out of our mouths.

"Yes they did and yes you are." The teacher said. "They not only hear the other children call their parents Mommy and Daddy, they also know who you are by what you do for them." She said.

My husband and I were shocked. We had purposely called each other our names rather firmly in front of them so that it could not be said we taught them to call us anything other than our names. We went home and cautiously entered this new chapter with labels.

"It's not as if we can have a conversation with them and tell them we're not Mommy and Daddy. God is at work and at this point I'm trying to wrap my mind around this." I thought to myself.

Although we are walking in the role of parents doing all that comes under that job description, we've never thought of or planned for this because we were always trying so hard to stay in protection mode caring for these beauties until the biological parents were cleared by DSS.

Even though we stood our ground in the roles assigned by DSS for the purpose of reunification, as the caseworker stated, all I know is, as mentioned before, God truly has jokes. From that very first phone call,

He had a plan in motion, and His will is always fulfilled, no matter what.

We finally found out the reason we were asked to care for the girls, why DSS would not allow the babies to go home with the biological parents from the hospital. They needed to clean their house of mold, clean the carpets and create a safe space for the girls to sleep, stay and play.

After the visits ended, the biological parents told us it was taken time getting the house in order. Then it turned to they wanted the state to foot the bill and they were not trying to do that.

After months of that, I asked had they at least cleaned the house so the girls could have visits. There were so many reasons why they had not and or could not do what was requested by DSS. It became clear to us that they weren't trying to do the work needed to be done so they could be reunified with the girls.

We were in and out of court, listening to all the excuses why DSS wanted the girls reunified at the same time watching the actions of the biological parents, as well as listening to them express actions that showed they did not want reunification. And it was stated by the biological parents maybe after they've been potty trained the twins could come home with them.

Which now made us view the whole situation differently. We were loving, praying over, training, teaching, and parenting these beautiful little girls, for them to come in at what seems to be an easier age for them and then choose reunification, instead of preparing their home as required by DSS.

The caseworker still treated us as unpaid babysitters who only mattered as long as we had no questions, concerns, and or issues with what we saw and heard.

As the girls grew, they amazed us the love they shared with everyone they met. The kindness and the respect they showed to others also amazed us.

Chapter 8: the adoption that Wasn't

D biological mother had a lawyer, and then there was a uring this entire time, the girls had a lawyer and the

caseworker. Up until our last court date we had been going with what we were told from their caseworker.

Even though we had made numerous complaints about the caseworker, how the girls were treated, no financial assistance, and how do we change our agreement from helping with reunification to since all visitation had ended, as well as phone calls, to adopting the girls?

Fortunately, the caseworker that was over the girls' case leading us astray all this time was removed shortly before our last court appearance. The supervisor who had taken over spoke with us trying to get understanding on why weren't we receiving financial assistance? Why hadn't we requested adoption and after learning how we were treated she seemed upset.

"The girls have a lawyer and that's who you tell your request to." She said.

Whenever we went to court the girls' lawyer always requested we bring the girls to court with us. Although we did so, as soon as the hearing would start the girls started talking or laughing or making all kinds of noises, we were always asked to take the girls out of the room by the bailiff. I guess they were a disruption in the courtroom.

After our last time in court, it hit us, it could have possibly been the plan all along. Not only did we not know what was said. Although we had requested copies from the caseworker and the lawyer, of any and all court hearings with the girls we never received one.

At least we never received anything until the order that came forth during our last hearing, May 2015. Even though we had to shoot out a couple emails before we received that order we actually received it from the new DSS supervisor that was assigned to us who made sure we got a copy. I can't remember how many times I reached out to the lawyer before we received the copy.

Anyway, after speaking to the girls' lawyer, he asked us, what did we want to do? After we told him we'd like to adopt the girls, he led us to believe he was going to push for that. However, just like every other court visit, we were asked to take the girls out due to their joyful behavior.

Not long afterward we left the courtroom, the lawyer came into the room where we were, he was smiling so we began smiling.

"Did we win?" I asked.

He said yes, we were so happy. Until we heard, "you got full legal custody and guardianship." All smiles quickly left.

"What happened to our request for adoption?" I said, almost yelling.

"Oh the caseworker took it off the table." He responded.

So off I went to ask the caseworker, which was actually the supervisor who had newly been assigned, why she took adoption off the table, knowing that's what she and I discussed as the best option for the girls.

She looked at me and explained that she had nothing to do with it. It was the decision of the girls' lawyer and her job was to follow his decision for the girls as long as it was in the best interest for the girls.

"We've already discussed it, I thought it was the best decision for the girls." She concluded.

We were extremely upset. So of course I went right back to the lawyer and asked him why?

He looked at me like "What?"

"Why did you tell me the caseworker took it off the table when, in fact, it was your decision to take it off the table. The caseworker told me she follows your decision, unless it is not in the best interest of the child or children. And she actually thought we had changed our minds about adoption." I said

The lawyer then said "Oh did I say the caseworker? I meant the judge took it off the table."

I felt like I was jabbed straight in the heart. I asked him was there a way we could speak with the judge. After all, this was a different judge than the one that started out with the girls.

"No you can't. He retired and this was his last case." Was his response.

Although we were so disappointed about not being able to adopt the girls and legally become their parents, God had already begun a work

~ 34 ~

that no court, no lawyer, or shady caseworker on the face of this earth could ever shake!!!

After getting myself together, we packed the girls up and thanked the supervisor, who took over their case.   Even though the biological parents did not show up, I spoke to the biological mom's lawyer and asked what I needed to do to be able to adopt the girls. He told me it is now out of the state's hands; "adoption will have to be done solely by you."

"And it is an expensive task," He added.

"What if the biological parents said yes to the adoption?"I said as I took a deep breath.

He explained we would have to file paperwork with their signatures, agreeing to surrender custody, wait, and hope they don't change their minds within the time given by the court. And that will complete an adoption.

"Thank you." I appreciate it.

As we were leaving the courthouse, the supervisor walked out with us. Lo and behold, the biological parents are walking in, I suppose they were coming for the hearing that had ended. As always, I'm telling the girls to say hi to mom. For some reason, they would never call her mom or him dad. They would always call them by their names or should I say what sounds like their names. After all, when they used to come to the shop, they would tell them their names, which I thought was strange.

Up until the very day leaving the courthouse May 2015, it always hurt my heart, to hear the girls call them by name. And I would always try to teach them to be respectful to their biological parents. Until the Supervisor who helped me in a matter of days more than we have been helped since being introduced to DSS confronted me about the situation.

"Don't do that."She advised.

I turned and looked at her "What?" I asked her.

"I'm listening to you telling them to call them mom and dad." She said.

I told her I felt bad for them and I wanted to make sure they respect them for who they are.

"I understand." She said. "However, you have to understand, they do not know them as mom and dad. They know them as who they call them, which are their names. To these beautiful little ones you and your husband are Mommy and Daddy. Although you've told me that you and your husband feel a little strange because they have started calling you, Mommy and Daddy, you two are the ones they wake up to. You two are the ones they run to when afraid. You two are the ones who take care of them, kiss them, hug and love on them. And of course you two comfort them when they're sad, not feeling well, or they just want to be spoiled. They know who and what you are to them."

I can't even explain the feeling I had after hearing all of that and looking at the biological parents expressions when the girls call their names and they respond with *"hey twins, you're getting big."*

Looking so detached as if they weren't even their parents, as if they are relieved they are with us and they can now leave since the case is now closed with DSS.

Although what we can call the first phase of our God-given choice to choose our beautiful twins has come to a rest.

The funny thing is that strange feeling is no longer strange.

Conclusion: The Strange (Feeling) Emotion Identified

I with twins, a strange feeling showed up. When we were asked, n the beginning of this journey, when I was told she was pregnant

would we take care of the girls because they would not be allowed to go home with the biological parents, I also had that strange feeling. The feeling was not sad, it was not mad, and even after hearing the negative comments when I would discuss it, it definitely wasn't jealousy.

After all, what I do know is that only God can create and impregnate a life. And the same God that gives awesome blessings of beautiful babies to special individuals has no problem blessing me in a more awesome way. And although I came to realize this awesome fact, long before this journey ever began in our lives, jealousy has never been an emotion I'd claim or act on. I've trusted God in such a way it upset the balance of others during the majority of my life.

With that said, the emotion, or as I originally stated, the strange feeling I had in the beginning of this journey, which I could not describe, was actually ANTICIPATION. I believe an honest God-given anticipation from the depth of my soul was what I felt from the initial phone call.

According to Google, here are definitions of anticipation, a noun which means the action of something, expectation or prediction. It goes on to say a phrase of anticipation with the probability or expectation of something happening. Summed all up to the true meaning of anticipation, being excited, waiting eagerly for something you know is going to happen.

Anticipation is, "looking forward with excitement to what is coming, resting in the assurance that it will be good regardless of what form it takes." And most importantly, Google describes the spiritual meaning of anticipation "to be driven by the spirit of God to foresee, and act in advance" to "what is being brought to your attention."

Now I know that's a lot to take in. However, although the highlights of the journey documented were the happy times mixed with a few difficult and unfortunate times, there were times when we had family and friends come against us, thinking we were crazy for taking on this assignment with no type of assistance, no type of preparations, as well as after being mistreated by DSS.

However, what I learned about this strange feeling is for some reason I just couldn't shake it. And it had me continuing to move forward. When I started keeping notes in my journal with things that has now turned into writing this book, back in 2013, it started out as a traveling journal, writing little things down that I thought was special and/or noteworthy, thinking that one day the girls may want to read it when they were older and know their story.

To describe it now I would say I totally agree with our family friend: "God's going to do what He's going to do!"

Back in August 2011, while school shopping for our oldest two, I received the first phone call that started this assignment. Shortly after the biological mom's initial call, the biological dad called to ask me if I had been told. I let him know yes, she told me. He fussed a little bit and

~ 39 ~

before ending the call I told him, "Don't worry, God's got her." He mumbled something and hung up.

That feeling at this time I'd say may have been the size of the proverbial mustard seed. It was there, I felt it, but it was gone after each conversation.

As time went on, the biological mom called me in October or November 2011 to let me know she was having twins.

"Twins, that's awesome." I am so happy for you.

As she rubbed it in knowing as many did, I've always wanted twins. She ended that phone call and that feeling was back. It was a little bit stronger than before, and after the call I couldn't just shake it.

My conversation with God at this time was, ***OK God you really got jokes.*** I really didn't understand what was going on at this point. Now it's one of my babies having twins who really hasn't cared for her other children as she would have liked.

After speaking to our family friend and she confirming that "Yes, sometimes God is the best comedian."

She also said "Those are your twins."

After hearing that, that emotion is growing and now I'm feeling something I can't explain.

"You know what we've gone through. There's no way that family is going to let that happen." I said to her.

She called my name, told me to calm down. She let me know, she heard it clear as day. "God said those are your twins. God can do it however he wants to do it. If He wants to Bless you with twin babies and you don't have to gain a pound, than that's how He'll do it."

After that phone call ended, whatever that strange feeling, I couldn't shake it from that point on. Because I trusted this friend with my life, and I know her life is grounded in the Lord, I held what she said close to my heart. However, I had gone through so much with the biological mom's family, I was not holding my breath as they say.

In May 2012, I received a call from the biological mom letting me know she was in the hospital. She said, she had been there for a while. This was shortly before Mother's Day and they were keeping her there until she delivered her babies because her medication needed to be monitored.

I told her to listen to the doctors and take care of herself. I also told her God's got her and her babies. She thanked me for always talking to her like she's a normal person. And as always, I told her, "you are a normal person."

"Just because life and circumstances dealt you a hard blow, doesn't make you less of a beautiful person." I added.

Before the call ended, I reminded her, she was still my baby and I loved her. (Our history goes back decades.) The feeling was growing even more at this point. Approximately a month later I received a call from the biological mom letting us know she had had the babies and they were fraternal girls. And as you know, here is where our assignment officially began.

Although we have gone on an amazing roller coaster ride of trials, tribulations, and different emotions during this time, we've gone from the phone calls to the he say she say, and we've ended up in court.

And here we are fast forward to May 2015 as we prepared to leave the courthouse, the large echoed halls, leading to the cold, non-emotional courtrooms. Something we will not miss at all.

The joy in these little faces made all we've gone through so well worth it. We proceed out of the front doors, the girls staring at the metal detectors where the police officers serve, checking bags, scanning people and letting them know if they can enter.

We step outside of the courthouse, the first breath has been taken. ***Oh yes, thank you, Lord!***

These little girls are so excited as they always are when they locate the car; extra hugs and extra kisses as we buckle them into their car seats.

Once my husband and I are safely in our seatbelts, we were now ready to head home. And although we had decided months ago since we no longer saw the biological parents putting forth an effort to be reunited with the girls, we will be moving forward with adopting the girls and completing our family.

On the ride home, we discussed the desire to adopt again. Hubby was still on the fence, because he still had a notion that the biological parents may come through and he'd have to yet again standby and watch my heart break.

"No sir, not going to happen. I would love to have the adoption final before they go to school." I assured him.

"OK, that's what we'll work towards." He agreed.

At that moment, it hit me like a ton of bricks. The feeling that started as a tiny little thing, that grew and overtime took over my heart and some aspects of my life in such a unique and strange way ANTICIPATION.

Have I ever anticipated something before? Yes, I have, and it never felt like this. What God revealed to me was I was literally, in a sense, fighting the feeling, the emotion of anticipation.

Although I was in the third grade when the prayer I would be married and have twins before the rapture was prayed, in a sense I've anticipated this day for decades.

Hebrews 11:1 says, "Now faith is the substance of things hoped for, the evidence of things not seen." I put my heart's desire before God so long ago, I thought it would come one way, but God is God and he can give you the desires of your heart in the most dynamic and pure way one could ever imagine.

To sum it up, over the years I've sought God and believed God for many things. Although our family friend told me to stay calm and trust God, in my heart of hearts I was doing just that, but my head had me thinking about past difficulties and hurts that affected my heart so if something should derail what was to be, I would not get hurt.

After leaving the courthouse and realizing the totality of anticipation, we never looked back. From that day forward, these were officially our babies.

REFLECTION: What prayer have you buried that God is reminding you of? **SCRIPTURE:**

Therefore I say unto you, What things so ever ye desire, when ye pray, believe that ye receive them, and ye shall have them. Mark 11:24 (KJV)

PRAYER:

Father,

I thank You that You have all power, and You choose to breathe life into a request I had forgotten and thought was dead in my life. I thank You that You are challenging me to dig deep and believe again. To believe for more than I could ask or think. I believe that as I continue to speak words of faith You will do what only You can do and make things happen that I could never make happen.
In Jesus Precious name I pray.

Amen.

A Love Letter to OUR LuvBugs

Our　　　　　　　Precious　　　　　　　Girls,

Ourstorytogetherbeganinawaywecouldhaveneverplanned,but
onlyGodcouldhavewritten.Atfirst,weweresimplyaskedtohelp,to
stepinwhenyourparentscouldnot,togiveyouasafeplaceanda
steadyhand.Whatwedidn'tknowthenwasthatweweren'tjust
opening our home to you, we were opening our hearts forever.

The day you were placed in Daddy's
carriedthebiggestpieceofourhearts.Eachdaythatpassed,ourbond
grewdeeper,throughsleeplessnights,tinygiggles,littlesteps,and
whisperedprayers.Bythetimeyouturnedthree,thepapersmadeit
official,butourheartshadalreadyclaimedyoulongbefore.Youwere
ours from the very beginning, even before the world said so.

Youarenotjustourdaughters,youareourmiracle,ouranswered
prayer,ourproofthatlovemakesafamily.Thejourneywasn'talways
easy,buteverymomentledustothisbeautifultruth:webelongtoeach
other, forever.

Wepromisetoalwaysremindyouofwhereyoucamefrom,notasa
storyofloss,butasatestimonyofGod'sfaithfulnessandthe
unstoppablepoweroflove.Youwereneverunwanted,youwere
chosen, twice over. First by God, then by us.

Forever and Always,

With all our love,

Mommy&Daddy

"Coming Next"

In Our Hearts From the Start II

(As the journey of Love continues, there are hurdles we must climb and challenges we must overcome)

As we move forward our goal is now to adopt these beautiful little girls before they begin school. I would have never known this could be done ifa sweet kind attorney I met had not told me. Life is a little smoother.

Contact Website?

Landing Page: ItsDanettaMcDavid@gmail.com

itsDanettaMcDavid.com

www.ingramcontent.com/pod-product-compliance
Lightning Source LLC
Chambersburg PA
CBHW051559120626
46551CB00013B/1594